Venus

Earth

Asteroid Belt

Saturn

Neptune

A Look at Earth

A Look at Earth

John Tabak

Franklin Watts

A DIVISION OF SCHOLASTIC INC.
NEW YORK · TORONTO · LONDON · AUCKLAND
SYDNEY · MEXICO CITY · NEW DELHI · HONG KONG
DANBURY, CONNECTICUT

Photographs © 2003: Corbis Images/Paul A. Souders: 83, 105; Dembinsky Photo Assoc./Richard Hamilton Smith: 69, 102; Gary A. Glatzmaier, University of California, Santa Cruz, Earth Sciences Department: 27, 94; Hans-Peter Bunge, Princeton University: 24, 25, 88 (from "Nature", Vol. 379, pp. 436-438, 1 Feb. 1996); NASA: 78, 79 (JPL), 2, 10, 93; Phil Richardson, Woods Hole Oceanographic Institution: 63 (from "Science", Vol. 207, pp. 643-645); Photo Researchers, NY: 36, 37 (Lynette Cook/SPL), 41, 97 (Jack Fields), 81 (Geospace/SPL), 19 (David Hardy/SPL), 51, 109 (Bruce M. Herman), 45 (Institute of Ocenagraphic Sciences/NERC/SPL), 42, 43, 66 (NASA/Goddard Space Flight Center/SPL), 23 (Stephen and Donna O'Meara), cover (Erich Schrempp); Photri Inc.: 48, 84; The Image Works/Joe Carini: 20, 106; Visuals Unlimited: 72 (Bruce Berg), 32 (D. Cavagnaro), 75 (John D. Cunningham), 12, 13 (C.P. George), 58, 59, 101 (NASA/GSFC), 55, 98 (NASA/JPL), 15 (NGDC), 53 (Erwin Nielsen), 65 (NOAA).

The photo on the cover shows an illustration of Earth from the Moon with a starfield visible. The photo across from the title page shows Earth from outer space.

Library of Congress Cataloging-in-Publication Data

Tabak, John.
  A look at Earth / by John Tabak.
    p. cm. — (Out of this world)
Summary: An in-depth look at the earth's composition, environment, and biomes.
Includes bibliographical references and index.
  ISBN 0-531-12266-2 (lib. bdg.)   0-531-15583-8 (pbk.)
  1. Earth—Juvenile literature. [1. Earth.] I. Title. II. Out of this
world (Franklin Watts, Inc.)
  QE631.4 .T33 2003
  550—dc21   2002001728

1 2 3 4 5 6 7 8 9 10 R 12 11 10 09 08 07 06 05 04 03

FOR LEELA

A Look at Earth

Contents

When seen from outer space, it is easy to understand why Earth is sometimes called the "blue planet."

Chapter 1

Iron Sphere/ Metal Ocean

Orbiting our Sun at a distance of about 93 million miles (150 million km) is a solid iron sphere. It has a diameter of about 1,500 miles (2,450 km), which is about two-thirds the diameter of our Moon. It's bigger than the biggest asteroids in the solar system.

And while estimates of the sphere's temperature vary, everyone agrees that it's hot. Current estimates of the temperature of the sphere range from 7,200° F (4000° C) to 14,000° F (7800° C), which is hotter than the surface of the Sun. One thing that all scientists agree on is that the iron sphere does not melt. The pressures on the sphere are so extreme that even at these very high temperatures iron remains solid.

The pressure on the sphere is millions of times greater than the pressure of the atmosphere at Earth's surface.

As you might expect from an iron sphere it's also very massive. (*Mass* is the amount of material that makes up an object.) The mass of this sphere is equal to almost 10 percent of the mass of the entire Earth even though the volume of the sphere is less than 1 percent of Earth's total volume.

Finally, our sphere seems to revolve at almost—but not quite—the same speed as Earth. There is, however, some disagreement among scientists about the exact length of one day on the sphere. Accurate measurements are difficult to make. As best they can presently determine, it seems that every few hun-

dred years the giant iron sphere gains one 24-hour-day on us. The word "day" has a different meaning on the iron sphere, however, because it revolves in complete darkness.

Scientists have given this remarkable sphere a name. They call it the *inner core*. It's located at the center of our planet. No one's ever seen it. No one ever will. It's completely inaccessible. The temperatures near the center of our planet are too high to drill down into it and so are the pressures. To get a probe close to the sphere scientists would have to pass it through lots of rock and almost 1,400 miles (2,250 km) of molten iron and nickel. Our solid inner core is immersed in an ocean of molten metal called the *outer core*.

So how do we know that the inner and outer cores are there at all?

Earthquakes

Earthquakes gave one of the very first indications that the inner and outer cores existed. To understand how earthquakes can be used to study Earth's interior it helps to think about echoes.

Suppose that you entered a canyon that you had never seen before. And suppose that you entered the canyon on a moonless night so that even though you were now inside the canyon you still couldn't see it. You could learn about the shape of the canyon by yelling and listening to the echo of your own voice. If you heard the echo of a short word before you had even finished yelling the word, you'd know that one of the walls of the canyon was nearby. (If the wall were farther away, the echo would have required more time to return.) If you shouted one word but heard multiple echoes it would mean that there were several surfaces inside the canyon that had reflected your voice.

Wreckage in Anchorage, Alaska, is evidence of the force of the earthquake that struck there in 1964, one of the most powerful ever recorded in North America.

The Discovery of the Liquid Outer Core

Much of the energy that earthquakes release travels through our planet in the form of waves. These waves are grouped into two main types, primary waves and secondary waves, called P waves and S waves for short. Primary waves compress and expand the rock as they pass through them. When a secondary wave (also called a shear wave) passes through rock it momentarily changes the shape of the rock without changing the volume. The distinction between P waves and S waves is important because while P waves can travel through liquids, S waves cannot. That fact, some math, and a lot of seismometers are what scientists used to discover the liquid outer core.

The paths that P waves travel through the center of the planet are generally complicated ones, but P waves can travel through Earth's center. They can penetrate the core and be detected on the side of Earth opposite the location where the quake occurred. The same can't be said for S waves. S waves penetrate rock but they're damped out by liquids. Trying to pass an S wave through a liquid is a little like trying to bounce a ball on a pillow. As a consequence there's a large "shadow zone" for S waves on the side of Earth opposite the location of the quake. This S wave shadow zone is the seismic shadow cast by the liquid core. It's the region behind the outer core that the S waves couldn't penetrate. The size of the shadow zone indicates the size of the outer core. A small outer core would cast a small shadow zone. A large outer core would cast a large shadow. Earth's core, which is comprised of both the inner and outer cores, is roughly the size of the planet Mars. It casts a pretty big shadow. Precise measurements of the shadow zone and a little trigonometry are all that's necessary to compute the location of the boundary of the outer core.

The direction of the echoes would tell you something about the location of each wall. As you got better at analyzing the echoes you might notice that certain frequencies were reflected more strongly than others. Some frequencies of sound might be absorbed. This would tell you something about the smoothness of the canyon walls. If you regularly changed your position as you shouted and listened you could—

at least in theory!—collect enough information to draw a picture of the canyon without ever seeing it. You'd have a "sound portrait." You would have acquired all of the information for your canyon-portrait by hearing instead of seeing, but with enough mathematics and enough science you'd know as much about the shape of the canyon as if you had seen it in broad daylight.

This is the idea behind earthquake analysis. When a large earthquake occurs tremendous amounts of energy are released in the form of waves. Some of these waves move across the surface of the planet and cause buildings to tremble, utility poles to swing wildly back and forth, and plates and books to fall off shelves. Much of the energy, however, is directed downward and causes Earth's interior to vibrate. These waves can cause Earth to ring like a bell. It does ring like a bell. Our planet rings like a bell with a very complicated shape. There are many high frequency and low frequency pitches present in the ringing. Some of the frequencies fade out quickly but at certain frequencies our planet rings for a very long time. Earthquake waves at certain frequencies can echo back and forth through our planet for days after a major quake.

The paths earthquake waves travel through our planet are not simple ones. Earthquake waves travel at different speeds through granite than they do through solid iron. They travel through molten iron in still another way. They change direction as they travel from one region to another. Sometimes they're reflected at the boundaries that separate different types of material. And each time a wave speeds up or slows down or changes direction it picks up information about the structure of our planet. To discover the core, scientists learned to listen to the waves—in a way that's somewhat similar to the "sound picture" described above—and then they learned to analyze them.

Scientists have placed *seismometers,* devices for measuring earthquakes, all across the surface of our planet. These seismometers "listen" for the thousands of earthquakes, large and small, that occur each year. The measurements that they make are the measurements scientists analyze to obtain information about Earth's interior. Over the years, scientists have acquired more and better seismometers. They've become more adept at analyzing the information that the seismometers collect. In so doing, they've learned about a place that they can never hope to see, the interior of our planet.

Heat and Earth's Interior

Why are the inner core and outer core so hot? To answer that question we need to look at the ancient history of our planet. Earth has a fiery past. The Sun and planets of our solar system formed out of a single, huge cloud of gas and dust. That cloud became the Sun and planets. The material in the cloud slowly formed into individual bodies and these bodies began to contract under the force of their own gravity. The material in each body became compressed and the more it was compressed the hotter it became. Simultaneously, there were numerous collisions with other bodies—bodies that formed from the same cloud at the same time. These collisions also generated a great deal of heat as kinetic energy, the energy of motion, was converted into heat energy when the bodies smashed together. Slowly, the material that makes up Earth today began to accumulate

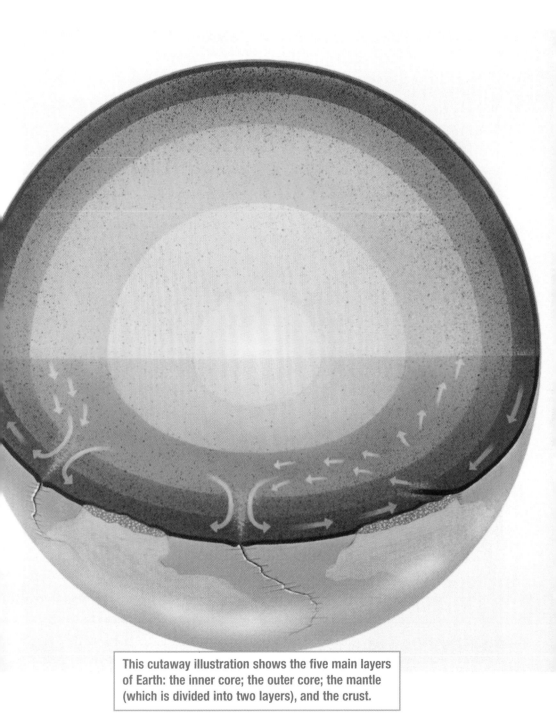

This cutaway illustration shows the five main layers of Earth: the inner core; the outer core; the mantle (which is divided into two layers), and the crust.

Volcanic eruptions demonstrate the immense energy and heat that are constantly at work beneath Earth's surface.

and then it began to melt. Heavier, denser materials settled further down inside each body while the lighter materials rose closer to the surface. All of that motion produced friction and even more heat. Earth's interior, and possibly even its surface, melted. There may have been huge, deep seas of molten rock sloshing about the surface. Then, slowly, Earth began to cool.

Earth is still cooling. Think about volcanoes. Volcanoes are like windows into Earth's interior. Each window gives us a slightly different view, but one thing that all volcanoes have in common is that everything that comes out of every one of them is incredibly hot. This is a little surprising because Earth has had almost five billion years to cool off. A pie taken out of a hot oven and placed on the counter will soon reach room temperature, but underneath its thin, cool, ancient crust Earth is still as hot as a volcano. Further down, it's even hotter.

In the nineteenth century scientists really thought of Earth as a sort of large, spherical, cooling pie. They thought that they could learn the age of Earth from its temperature. (To return to the pie analogy, if you knew the temperature of the pie when it was removed from the oven, and you knew the rate at which it cooled, you could discover how long the pie had been out of the oven by taking its temperature.) These scientists imagined Earth as a huge, molten sphere because they were already familiar with some of the simpler aspects of the theory of planetary formation described above. To them the problem of determining Earth's age from its current average temperature seemed fairly straightforward. First, they needed a reasonable estimate of Earth's initial temperature. Next, they needed information about the elements of which our planet is composed, and then, finally, they computed the rate at which any molten sphere with Earth's characteristics would cool. To check their work they compared their computations with their best estimate of Earth's present temperature.

The most famous attempt at estimating the age of Earth from its temperature was made by the British scientist and mathematician William Thomson (1824-1907), also known as Lord Kelvin. Kelvin was fascinated by the ideas involved, and he thought about the problem off and on for decades. In his last estimate, made near the end of his life, he assumed that the initial temperature of a huge, molten Earth would be about 2200° F (1200° C). By computing the rate at which heat would escape through the crust and into space, he estimated that our planet could be no more than 24 million years old. He believed that if Earth were much older than that, it would also be much cooler.

Lord Kelvin was right about Earth radiating heat into space, but he was wrong about its age. We now know that Earth is much older than 24 million years. It's about 4.6 billion years old. And we understand the mistake that Lord Kelvin made. Kelvin was unfamiliar with *radioactivity*. (We say a material is radioactive when the atoms of which the material is composed break apart or decay spontaneously. When this occurs heat is released.) Most of Kelvin's work on the age of Earth was completed well before the most basic properties of radioactive materials were identified. The reason that radioactivity is important to Kelvin's problem of estimating Earth's age is that there are radioactive elements inside Earth. That's what keeps the interior warmer than it would otherwise be. Our planet doesn't cool passively like a pie on a counter; it stays hot because it has its own heater, the

Lava flows from Kilauea volcano in Hawaii. Lava is molten rock from beneath Earth's crust. When it is still underground, this rock is known as magma.

radioactive elements present inside it.

What's the effect of all that heat? One consequence is motion in the liquid outer core. The reason is that the heat in the outer core isn't evenly distributed. Some parts are hotter than others. The outer core is further warmed at the surface of the inner core and as the liquid is warmed it expands and becomes more buoyant than the liquid above it. (These kinds of currents are sometimes called *density-*

This illustration is a convection model of Earth's mantle showing differences in temperature. The coolest temperatures are those in shades of blue, while the warmest are those in shades of red. The yellow and green regions are in the middle, with yellow representing warmer temperatures.

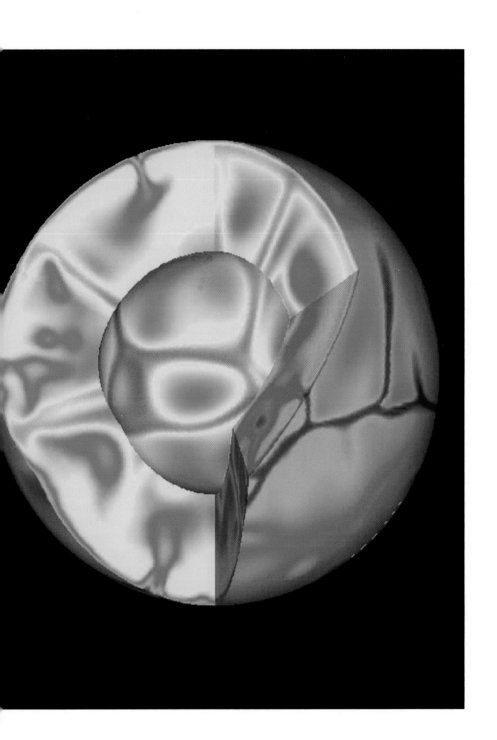

Scientists interested in studying Earth's magnetic field have a difficult time studying it in the laboratory. The temperatures and pressures that exist in the outer core, where the magnetic field originates, are extremely difficult to reproduce experimentally. The pressures inside the inner core are millions of times greater than Earth's atmospheric pressure. Duplicating these pressures poses a severe challenge for even the most imaginative and well-funded scientists. Reproducing the changes in Earth's magnetic field is even harder, and Earth's magnetic field changes constantly. The most remarkable change occurs every few hundred thousand years when the north magnetic pole and the south magnetic pole "flip flop" or exchange places. So even if scientists could find a reasonable experiment to duplicate the conditions that exist in the outer core, it would be impossible to watch the experiment evolve over many thousands of years to see if the experiment accurately reproduced Earth's complicated and fluctuating magnetic field. For these reasons many scientists use computer modeling to study Earth's magnetic field.

Developing a computer model of Earth's magnetic field begins with the measurements gathered near Earth's surface and the equations that are thought to describe the conditions in the vicinity of the outer core. The goal is to create a "virtual Earth," a numerical simulation of the real thing. They then compare the behavior of the virtual magnetic field with what they know of Earth's own magnetic field. If the agreement is good this indicates that the theories that scientists have developed to describe what happens deep in Earth's interior may be correct.

Beginning in 1996 scientists began publishing the results of very large-scale simulations of Earth's magnetic field and the motions deep within our planet that generate it. The equations the scientists used were solved repeatedly—the output of one set of calculations was used as the input for the next set—with the goal of simulating how the magnetic field changes over the course of hundreds of thousands of years. The solutions are in reasonably good agreement with what scientists know about Earth's magnetic field. The virtual magnetic fields had strengths that were similar to the strength of Earth's magnetic field and the virtual north and south magnetic poles flip-flopped in a way that's similar to the flip-flops known to have occurred during Earth's past. Surprisingly, these computations also indicated that Earth's inner core rotates at a rate that's slightly faster than the rate at which Earth's surface rotates. This was a stunning and unexpected result that prompted scientists to return to their original data to search for evidence to support this computer-generated prediction. Many scientists believe that they've found evidence for this surprising and difficult-to-explain phenomena, called "super-rotation," in the measurements that they collected on and near Earth's surface.

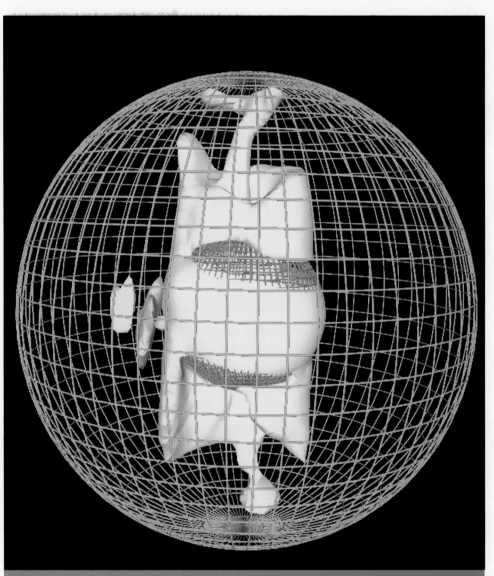

This is a computer simulation illustrating the swirling flow of liquid iron in Earth's interior. The movement of this liquid creates Earth's magnetic flow and has been characterized by scientists as a kind of "geodynamo."

driven currents. An object's density is the ratio of its mass to its volume. As heat moves from the inner core into the outer core, the volume of the heated liquid increases—it's mass doesn't change—and so it becomes less dense. Density-driven currents are the result of density differences in the fluid.) As less dense, more buoyant material at the bottom of the outer core expands, it begins to rise towards the upper boundary of the outer core. Eventually, it cools and descends back towards the inner core to begin the cycle again. These up-and-down motions are further complicated by the fact that all of this takes place inside a rotating "container," which, of course, is Earth itself, so that more than 1,800 miles (2,900 km) below our feet the outer core churns along 24 hours a day, seven days a week, year after year after year.

No one has ever seen these currents, of course, and so the question arises, "How do we know the currents exist at all?" One indication that currents exist in the outer core has to do with Earth's magnetic field, the same magnetic field that causes compass needles to point northward. An electric field is generated by the flow of an electrically conducting liquid. (Both iron and nickel, which make up most of the outer core, conduct electricity.) Scientists think it's the motion of these molten metals and the electrical currents that they generate that are responsible for creating Earth's magnetic field.

The chaotic motions of the outer core generate a magnetic field that's not very stable. The locations of Earth's magnetic poles drift a little each year, and every few hundred thousand years the north and south magnetic poles exchange places. All of this is thought to result from the complicated and disordered motions that occur in the outer core.

Computer Modeling and Earth's Interior

Scientists use computers to investigate the core of our planet, but they don't begin with computers. They begin with measurements and mathematics.

Scientists require lots of precise measurements to understand the interior of Earth, but the most valuable measurements—the ones taken directly from deep inside our planet—are impossible to make. Scientists can't directly observe the conditions deep inside Earth. The temperatures are extremely high. The pressures are unimaginable and, of course, there's all that rock. It blocks our view.

What scientists can do is make lots of surface measurements. They can make many additional measurements from outer space using satellites. The measurements they make from Earth's exterior are chosen to help them better understand Earth's interior. They measure gravity, for example, because information about the strength of Earth's gravity allows them to determine the amount and distribution of Earth's mass. The stronger the gravitational force exerted by a body, the greater its mass. What they found is that for its size Earth is a very massive object when compared to other bodies in the solar system. This kind of information allows them to determine which elements are abundant deep inside Earth.

As we've already mentioned, scientists also make lots of earthquake measurements because this type of measurement enables them to better understand the structure of our planet. Earthquake measurements are especially valuable for determining the geometry of Earth's interior. Taken together, earthquake measurements and gravitational measurements can give scientists insight into the structure and composition of our planet.

At first, however, these measurements are just numbers. The numbers themselves are not enough. Science isn't really about collecting numbers, it's about what those numbers mean. That's where mathematics comes into play.

Over the years, scientists have developed mathematical equations that they believe describe the interior of Earth. These equations reflect their best understanding of how materials behave under the tremendous temperatures and pressures that exist deep in Earth's interior. The equations are, however, very general. They can be used to describe the interior of Earth or the interior of another planet. By themselves, the equations, like the measurements, are not enough. In order to make the equations apply specifically to Earth, scientists incorporate the measurements made at and above Earth's surface into the solutions of the equations. The solutions link our understanding of the exterior with predictions about the interior of our planet. The equations are like a bridge between the measurements and their meanings. Unfortunately, these equations are very difficult to solve, and that's where computers come in to play.

Scientists use computers to generate accurate solutions to these equations. The computers need to be extremely powerful because the solutions are so complex. To develop detailed solutions the computers must perform planet-sized calculations. Only the fastest computers have a chance of finishing these calculations before the scientists grow old and retire.

When the computers finish their calculations, scientists compare the computer's solutions with the data that they've collected on how Earth actually behaves. The better the agreement, the more confidence they have in their assumptions and in their theories.

Good agreement with the data doesn't actually prove that a theory is correct, of course, but when computer models and data don't agree, scientists can be sure that something needs to be improved. Computer modeling has become a very important tool for scientists who are interested in finding out what makes Earth Earth.

These metamorphic rocks in the inner gorge of the Grand Canyon are an estimated 2 billion years old.

Chapter 2

From the Inside Out

When scientists describe something as a liquid they mean that it flows. When we think of liquids, we usually think of things like water and milk. These liquids don't just flow, they flow quickly. (When you tip over a glass of milk, it flows out so fast that it's all over the table before you can stop it.) But other materials can properly be described as liquids even though you'll never see them flow. Pitch, for example, is a sticky, dark substance obtained from wood or coal. At room temperature it's usually described as a solid, because when you look at it, you don't see it flow. You can't see it flow, but it flows as surely as water and milk flow. All you have to do is push gently on the pitch. It immediately begins to flow, but it does so at a much slower rate than milk or water. Pitch flows so slowly that the whole time it's flowing it feels solid. But flow it does. If you push long enough you can see the results of all that slow-motion flow.

The flows that occur deep inside Earth are often slower and stickier and harder for us to imagine than the sorts of flows that we see everyday. The pressures and temperatures that exist deep inside our planet cause materials to behave in ways that are outside our ordinary experience. Because materials deep within Earth are described as liquids, that doesn't mean that they flow in ways that we would immediately recognize as fluid, but, like pitch, they can and do flow. This must be kept in mind as we describe the structure of Earth.

Deep inside our planet, directly beneath our feet, rock is flowing. Like liquids, solids also behave differently deep inside Earth than they behave at the surface. The higher temperatures and pressures deep underground make all the difference. On Earth's surface solid rock isn't just solid, it's often strong and usually a little brittle. You can't bend it without breaking it. But deep inside Earth where the pressures and temperatures are very high, rock can be both solid and flexible. At certain temperatures and pressures, rock no longer behaves like "ordinary" rock. It hasn't melted yet, but it can bend without breaking. It's still heavy and in some ways it's still what we'd think of as "rock-like," but it's also very different than surface rock. Under higher temperatures and pressures rock will bend and twist, and given enough time it will, like pitch, flow. Part of understanding the interior of our planet means putting aside our old notions of solids and liquids and extending our imaginations so that we can visualize new ways for old familiar materials to behave.

A Layered Earth

Some of the same ideas and technologies that are used to investigate the inner core are used to investigate the other regions of Earth's interior as well. Scientists have discovered that each region completely surrounds the region beneath it and is completely surrounded by the one above it. Earth's structure is a little like that of an onion: peel back one layer and there's another one beneath it. The transition between one layer and another is fairly thin and easy to identify. In the center of everything, of course, is the inner core.

Surrounding the liquid outer core is a thin, uneven transition layer. The thickness of the transition layer varies, but it's never more than a few hundred miles, and sometimes it's much less. On the other side of this transition layer is the lower mantle. The lower mantle is made up mostly of minerals that contain the elements silicon, magnesium, calcium, oxygen, aluminum, and iron. Like the outer core, the lower mantle is about 1,400 miles (2,250 km) thick. It's rock, but it's not like the kind of rocks we find on the surface. This rock is very hot and very dense. It's squeezed by the weight of all the rock above them.

The lower mantle flows. Like the material called pitch, which was described at the beginning of this chapter, the lower mantle seems solid enough over short periods of time, but over the course of many years the lower mantle will slowly flow in great *convection cells*. Convection cells are circular currents that result from unequal heating. They're density-driven flows: Heat, which always flows from hot to cold regions, flows from the warmer outer core into the cooler lower mantle. The rock near the bottom of the lower mantle expands as it

warms. As it expands it becomes more buoyant than the rock above it and it begins to rise. As it rises it begins to cool and eventually sinks back to the mantle/core boundary region where the cycle repeats. If this sounds familiar, it should. We've already seen that currents in the

Earth's innermost core (solid yellow) is mostly solid iron and nickel. The outer core (spotted yellow) is liquid iron and nickel. The mantle (orange) is molten rock. The thinnest layer, the crust (blue), is about 6.2 miles (10 km) thick under the ocean and almost 19 miles (30 km) thick under the continent.

outer core arise in essentially the same way.

It's another 400 miles (650 km) from the top of the lower mantle to the surface. Most of that region is occupied by the *upper mantle*. There's a thin transition layer between the lower mantle and the upper mantle and then the upper mantle stretches almost all the way to the surface. The distance between Earth's surface and the upper mantle varies, but the upper mantle is never very far away. The upper mantle is generally less than about 4.5 miles (7 km) below the ocean floor. In some places it's even closer. To reach the upper mantle from the continents we'd have to drill somewhat deeper, but usually no more than about 25 miles (40 km). (It's a little bit deeper than this under tall mountains.) The upper mantle is thought to be made of the same sorts of elements as the lower mantle, but there's a difference. Unlike the regions that exist below it, we have some samples of the uppermost regions of the upper mantle. Nothing below the upper mantle has ever been sampled directly.

Besides the thin crust on which we live, the upper mantle is the only region that we can sample directly. We obtain samples of the upper mantle by analyzing the material that's made its way to the surface. Scientists, for example, study the material that flows out of volcanoes for clues about the chemical composition of the upper mantle. We can't drill down to the upper mantle. The deepest hole ever drilled in Earth's crust is a little over 7 miles (12 km) deep, and that hole, drilled by the former Soviet Union, was very difficult and very expensive to make. The best we can do is wait for the upper mantle to come to us.

Like the lower mantle the upper mantle is made of rock that flows very slowly. The currents in the upper mantle are also density-driven flows, and, like those in the lower mantle, these flows are organized into convection cells. (Heat from the warmer lower mantle flows into the cooler upper mantle and causes the material at the bottom of the upper mantle to expand and become more buoyant than the material above. Slowly—we'd measure its motion in centimeters per year—the material of the upper mantle begins to rise. Eventually, it cools and sinks to begin the cycle again.) The flows that develop in the upper mantle are similar in many ways to the flows that develop in the lower mantle, except for the shape of the flows. The big difference between the convection cells in the lower mantle and those in the in the upper mantle is geometric. The convection cells in the lower mantle are deep and those in the upper mantle are thought to be shallow. Convection cells in the upper mantle are no more than 400 miles (650 km) deep but some are more than ten times that wide. They circulate unimaginably slowly in massive oblong currents beneath Earth's surface.

On top of the churning upper mantle and surrounding everything else is the solid layer on which we live. It's called the crust.

The Crusty Truth

The crust is solid, but that doesn't begin to convey how dynamic a region the crust is. For centuries scientists have known that tremendous, almost unimaginable changes, have occurred in Earth's crust. They knew this long before they learned the cause of the changes. They knew it because they had made a few simple observations and they understood a little about what those observations meant about the nature of Earth's crust.

The first of these observations is almost too simple to make, but it's what the observation means that's important to our story. This first observation is that water flows down hills, not up, and that trees, rocks, and everything else that's solid tumble down as well. Nothing ever tumbles up. One important consequence of this simple observation is that over very long periods of time, mountains wear down, they don't "wear up." So given enough time there should be no mountains left. Given enough time all mountains should wear right down to their roots. All valleys should fill up with the soil and the rubble that washes down from the sides of the mountains. They should fill up with the rocks that tumble down from the mountain peaks. On a planet where erosion is the only force affecting the landscape, the surface of the entire planet should eventually be as smooth and as flat as the state of Kansas in the United States or the plains of Patagonia in Argentina.

But Earth's surface isn't that smooth. There are the great, gently rolling mountain ranges like the Appalachian Mountains in the eastern U.S. and the Snowy Mountains in eastern Australia. And there are mountains with sharp jagged peaks like those in the Himalayas, of which Mount Everest is a part, and the Andes Mountains of South America and the Alps in Europe. These mountains aren't just tall, they're often pointy and they're separated by deep V-shaped valleys. Erosion should have smoothed those points down long ago and filled in those V-shaped valleys. It hasn't happened yet, so there must be some other force besides erosion that acts on the landscape, a sort of anti-erosion force. That's the force that builds up what erosion tears down. For a long time no one knew what that force was.

The second observation that these early scientists made was that high on the peaks of these mighty mountains one could often find marine fossils. The 19th-century British naturalist Charles Darwin traveled the world as young man and wrote a book about his experiences entitled *The Voyage of the Beagle*. (The *Beagle* was the name of the ship on which he traveled.) He writes repeatedly about finding fossil beds, filled with the fossils of marine creatures, high in the Andes Mountains, more than two miles (3 km) above sea level! What force, he wondered, could have lifted enormous, and enormously heavy, layers of rock from the bottom of the Pacific Ocean to the peaks of some of the tallest mountains in the world? (We now know that even the summit of Mount Everest is made of rocks that formed beneath the sea.)

In the years since Darwin traveled the world, scientists have discovered that Earth's crust is cracked into big pieces that geologists call plates. The plates come in different shapes and sizes and together they

A sharp, isolated rock pyramid with steep, narrow ridges jutting from surrounding glaciers, the Matterhorn, in the Swiss Alps, is one of the world's most famous mountain peaks.

In this satellite image of Earth, the colors are very close to how the planet actually appears from space.

cover the entire surface of the planet except at some thin "seams" where material from the upper mantle wells up to fill in the gaps. These plates move slowly across Earth's surface, and, like cars on an impossibly crowded freeway, they continually scrape and collide with one another. When two cars collide at low speeds crumpled fenders can be the result. When two plates collide the result is sometimes a crumpled crust. We call those sections of crumpled crust mountain ranges. Scientists now recognize that it's the scraping and colliding of Earth's great plates that we experience as earthquakes. It's the collision of plates that causes the formation of mountain ranges. The force that

moves the plates is the main force that counteracts the smoothing force of erosion. This theory, called *plate tectonics*, is now one of the great unifying ideas in contemporary geology.

The Big Picture

Plate tectonics is a fairly new idea. It didn't gain widespread acceptance until the 1960's, although one scientist, the German meteorologist and geologist Alfred Wegener (1880-1930), had deduced parts of the idea by 1915.

Like anyone who studies a map of the world for a few hours, Wegener noticed that the eastern coast of South America fits almost perfectly against the western coast of Africa. (To achieve the fit we need to rotate South America counterclockwise a little and then move it all the way across the Atlantic Ocean.) Wegener also investigated other widely separated landmasses that seemed to fit when moved next to one another. In each case he discovered that not only did each pair of landmasses share a common geometry, they shared a common geology. The mineral deposits and geological formations at corresponding locations matched. He even discovered that similar types of fossils were present at corresponding points of landmasses that were now separated by great oceans. Wegener was driven to the remarkable conclusion that the continents are in motion. He hypothesized that they plowed through the rock of the ocean basins like ships through water.

Wegener's research didn't change many minds during his lifetime. One problem was that he couldn't suggest a mechanism capable of driving entire continents about Earth's surface like boats on a pond. More importantly, some of the most remarkable evidence that Earth's surface is in continual motion lies under the oceans and hidden from view. Wegener's theory is known as "continental drift." It isn't quite the theory of plate tectonics, but for about half a century Wegener's theory was the best explanation available to account for the remarkable fits that any one of us can observe on any world map today.

By the early 1960's scientists had the technology necessary to map the ocean floor in detail. What they learned is that some of the mightiest of Earth's features exist in perpetual darkness. These features are miles beneath the surface of the oceans. Many of these ridges and mountains and trenches were previously unknown, because no one could see them. As technology improved, scientists built up detailed "sound pictures" of these huge features using sonar. One thing these sonar measurements revealed is an enormous ridge twisting across the surface of our planet. The ridge divides the Atlantic ocean in two, but it doesn't stop there. Instead, this Atlantic ridge, which they called the *Mid-Atlantic Ridge*, is just part of a system of interconnected ridges that wind around the surface of our planet for a total of about 45,000 miles (75,000 km). It's one of our planet's largest features, yet almost the entire system lies in perpetual darkness, unseen and unseeable, at the bottom of Earth's oceans.

Special underwater imaging equipment, known as TOBI (Towed Ocean Bottom Instrument), created this image of the Reykjanes Ridge, an underwater mountain range south of Iceland in the north Atlantic Ocean.

But scientists didn't just measure the size and position of the Mid-Atlantic Ridge, they also measured the age of the sea floor on either side of it. These were the measurements that indicated what was happening at the ridge itself. Scientists discovered that the further away from the ridge they moved, the greater the age of the rocks that made up the sea floor. This was true whether one measured westward from the ridge (and so toward North and South America) or eastward from the ridge (and toward Europe and Africa). The youngest areas of the sea floor were always those that lay closest to the center of the ridge. The oldest sections were always furthest away.

The conclusion? Sea floor was being created at the ridge. As the sea floor spread away from the ridge, the eastern shore of the Atlantic moved further and further from the western shore. New sea floor was being created at the center of the Atlantic ocean!

Scientists have actually descended down to the heart of the Mid-Atlantic Ridge in research submarines. They've seen molten rock oozing up through the center of the ridge. From their submarines they can't get a good view of the entire ridge because it's much too big and it's much too dark at the bottom of the ocean. Observing the Mid-Atlantic Ridge through a window on a submarine is like observing the Grand Canyon at night with a flashlight. You can see a little, but not enough. In any case, they've taken pictures of lava flowing up through cracks in the sea floor. They've seen new ocean floor being created, but there's a problem. Earth's total surface area doesn't change. Earth remains a sphere. It doesn't change size so its surface area can't change, either. You can't just create surface. As new surfaces are created in some places, old surfaces must be destroyed in others. Earth's surfaces are destroyed in regions that scientists call *subduction zones.*

Subduction zones are found near the deepest trenches on Earth. These trenches extend further down below sea level than Mount Everest extends upward above it. At a subduction zone one plate slowly plunges down into the upper mantle as another plate overrides it. The lower plate descends beneath the upper one, and as the lower plate slips into the upper mantle it begins to heat up. Some of the heated material mixes with material from the upper mantle and is forced back up toward the surface to appear again later in the lava of volcanic eruptions.

And what of the forces that drive all of this motion? Scientists think that the plates are dragged along the surface of the planet by the great convection cells located in the upper mantle. These currents of rock churn steadily and with unimaginable slowness over huge expanses of time. They're density-driven currents, and they are what cause the plates to move. When plates collide at subduction zones the cooler, denser oceanic plate sinks into the warmer, less dense upper mantle. There is now some evidence that the crust sinks even further and plunges hundreds of miles down to slice into the lower mantle.

Why do the oceanic plates sink but not the continents? The answer, again, has to do with the relative density of the two regions. The continents are preserved because relative to the oceanic plates, continental rock is lighter and more buoyant. The continents can be battered by the forces of plate tectonics, but they can't be sunk.

Maps now exist that show the location of Earth's volcanoes, the location of earthquakes, and the boundaries of the plates that make up Earth's surface. When all of this information appears on one map it's easy to see that most earthquakes and volcanoes occur near the plate boundaries. This tremendous amount of data only makes sense with the help of the theory of plate tectonics.

The extent of the Pacific Ocean can be clearly seen in this image of Earth taken from space. The variation in depth of the oceans can be detected in the difference of colors.

Chapter 3

The
Oceans

Earth is a planet of oceans. This observation conflicts with the everyday experience of most of us. Most of us spend all of our time on land. We walk on it. We drive on it. We build on it. We live on it. Many of us go days or even years without seeing an ocean. On those occasions when we do see an ocean, we usually see just the edge of it. It's easy to forget how big the oceans are.

In terms of size, nothing else on the surface of our planet compares with the Pacific Ocean. The Pacific Ocean covers a greater area than all seven continents combined. The numbers speak for themselves:

- area of the Pacific Ocean: 64,210,000 square miles (166,240,000 square kilometers)

- area of all seven continents combined: 58,130,000 square miles (150,550,000 square kilometers).

The Pacific Ocean is the biggest single feature on the surface of our planet.

But it's more than size and water that distinguishes the oceans from the continents.

The maximum age of the oceanic crust—that's the land at the bottom of the ocean—is only about 200 million years. Most of the rock that makes up the ocean basins is even younger. By contrast, there are certain areas of North America where it's not difficult to find continental rock that's about 2 *billion* years old. The oldest continental rocks have been dated at about 4 billion years. To see why, look at the map that shows the plate boundaries and the zones of sea floor spreading. It's oceanic crust that's created at the ridge system, of which the Mid-Atlantic Ridge is just a part, and its oceanic crust that's destroyed at the subduction zones. It takes about 200 million years to completely replace all old ocean floor with new ocean floor.

And the ocean basins are different in still another way. They are much, much lower in elevation than the continents. Freshwater lakes—with the exception of the extremely deep Lake Baikal in Russia—are relatively shallow depressions. They fill with water because, despite their beauty, they're just regions of poor drainage. Very few freshwater lakes have a maximum depth of even 1,000 feet (300 m). By contrast, the average depth of the oceans is more than 12,000 feet (3,600 m).

The transition region between continent and ocean basin is very narrow. Each continent is surrounded by a *continental shelf* that slopes gently down. The shelf is really a part of the continent to which it

The limestone cliffs at Mather Point in the Grand Canyon are one of the most beautiful sights on Earth. From this vantage point, the floor of the canyon is about a mile down. The average depth of the oceans is twice that.

adheres. It's made of continental rock, which is less dense than the rock found in the ocean basins. Generally, the continental shelf is just a few tens of miles wide. In some places it's much less. It ends abruptly when the land plunges steeply to the ocean basin below.

The landscape of the ocean basins lies in permanent darkness and is under extreme pressure due to the miles of water piled high above it. It is in every way a much bigger place that what we see topside. For example, the tallest mountain on Earth isn't Mount Everest. Mount Everest is "only" about 29,000 feet (8,850 m) tall. The biggest mountain on Earth is Mauna Kea in Hawaii, which, when measured from base to summit, is 32,000 feet (9,750 m) tall. That's more than half a mile (0.8 km) higher than Everest. The reason Mauna Kea is less famous than Everest is that most of Mauna Kea is submerged beneath the sea. Most of it is underwater and in the dark. And it's not just the mountains of the ocean basins that are bigger. The deepest of the ocean's trenches, the subduction zones, are wider and deeper than any land canyon. The land beneath the seas is a different world from the surface of the seven continents that towers miles above them.

And, of course, there's the water.

The Water

The ocean basins, which are miles deep and thousands of miles wide, are filled to overflowing with water. But unlike water in a bucket, which can remain motionless for hours or even days at a time, the oceans are continually moving. They flow horizontally and vertically, quickly and slowly, and over distances large and small. On the small end are the gentle waves that lap at the piers and along harbor beaches

Waves wash over the bow of this observation ship in heavy seas off the coast of Antarctica.

when the weather is calm. Somewhat larger than these tiny waves are the slowly whirling masses of water that can be seen in satellite photographs. These can be 100 miles (160 km) or more in width and swirl across the face of the ocean for many months before disappearing. But these eddies are just medium-sized currents. On the large end are ocean currents that course through the open seas, some with far more capacity than all of the world's rivers combined. These big currents can flow for thousands of miles and for thousands of years and they can have profound effects on global weather patterns. It's to the cause of these motions that we now turn our attention.

Surface Currents and the Sun

Surface currents, a term that includes most of the currents that occur within about 1,300 feet (400 m) or so of the oceans' surface, are driven by the winds. Far to sea there are big regions of the oceans where the wind blows almost continuously, and almost always in the same direction. Those winds are caused by unequal heating of our planet's surface. Because Earth's surface is curved, not every region on the illuminated part of our planet receives the same amount of sunlight. When the sun is high in the sky over a region, that area receives bright, direct light and consequently more heat from the sun. In areas where the sun is low in the sky—either at sunrise or sunset or in regions near the north or south poles—it shines less directly on the surface. Those less illuminated regions receive less solar energy than regions where the Sun shines from directly overhead. Remember, too, that only half of the planet receives sunlight at any given time. Dark regions are rotated to face the Sun at sunrise and illuminated regions are rotated into darkness at sunset.

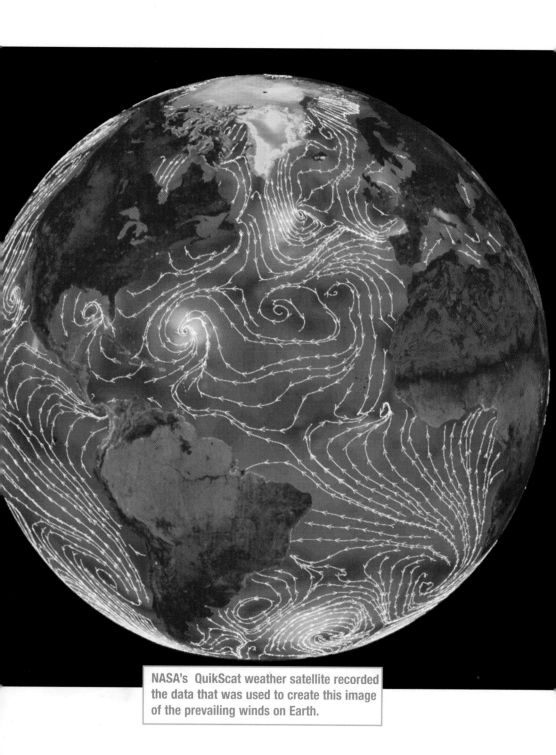

NASA's QuikScat weather satellite recorded the data that was used to create this image of the prevailing winds on Earth.

Here's one chain of events that results from unequal heating of Earth's surface:

- Unequal heating causes differences in air temperature at Earth's surface.

- These differences in air temperature are accompanied by differences in air pressure.

- Differences in air pressure cause the winds to blow. (Regions of high pressure air blow into low pressure regions.)

- As the winds sweep across the surface of the ocean they cause the surface waters to flow.

It's the Sun that drives the winds and it's the winds that drive the surface currents.

The effects of unequal heating of Earth's atmosphere might seem like they should be short-term in nature. It might seem that winds would develop and dissipate over a few hours or (at most) a few weeks. Sometimes it happens just that way. The air and water currents form and then die away, but it doesn't always happen that way. We'll soon see that there are other regions of the ocean where the winds have driven massive currents for thousands of years.

Large Currents and Earth's Rotation

Earth's rotation also has an effect on the direction of many of the ocean's currents, but it doesn't affect every current. To see why, imagine yourself on the deck of a ship far out at sea. From your position on the deck, the ocean looks flat. It's not, of course. It can't be flat. The ocean adheres to the surface of our spherical planet, but our planet is so large and its curve so gentle that over short distances it doesn't look curved at all. Over short distances, currents flow as if they were moving over a flat, non-rotating surface. Over long distances, however, it's an entirely different matter.

To see how Earth's rotation affects large ocean currents, it's important to understand just how fast we're moving even when we're standing still. Earth completes one turn about its axis of rotation every 24 hours. That means that even when we remain in place, each of us travels along a circular path centered on Earth's axis of rotation and that we, too, complete one turn every 24 hours. The *speed* with which we circle our planet's axis depends on our latitude. People at the equator travel the fastest because they have the furthest to go. They're about 3,960 miles (6375 km) from the axis and they travel eastward at a rate of about 24,000 miles (38,600 km) each day in a path that coincides with the equator. (The distance around our planet at the equator is roughly 24,000 miles (38,600 km).) Another way of saying the same thing is that someone standing on the equator is traveling about 1,000 miles per hour (1,600 kph) every hour of every day. A quick look at a globe will show that every other line of latitude—which you can see is actually a circle—is shorter than the equator. So if we're located north or south of the equator we travel more slowly about the axis of rotation than our neighbors at the equator. In fact, the closer we get to the north or south poles, the smaller the circular path we travel. It still takes us 24 hours to complete the circuit; we just don't need to travel as fast to go all the way around. By way of example, someone standing

Hurricane Floyd builds up strength over the Atlantic Ocean between Florida and the island of Cuba in September 1999, as shown in this photograph taken from space by a weather satellite.

at latitude 45° N travels eastward in a circle about Earth's axis at a speed of about 730 mph (1,180 kph). Someone standing at the north or south geographic pole is simple spinning at a rate of one turn per day without ever changing position relative to Earth's axis.

Suppose, now, that we place a powerful cannon at the equator and prepare to fire northward. Even before we fire the cannon, the shell, like the cannon, is already traveling eastward at a speed of 1,000 mph (1,600 kph) in a circle centered on Earth's axis of rotation. Firing the cannon due north doesn't change the shell's eastward velocity. Once fired, the shell will simply travel northward at the speed at which it was fired while it simultaneously travels eastward at 1,000 mph (1,600 kph). What's important for our story is that any point north of the equator travels eastward at a rate slower than that of the shell.

If we could ride on the shell that we fired northward, we'd get the impression that we were veering "off course," because although the cannon had been fired due north, our path would drift east of our original longitude. Why? The ground under us would be turning just fast enough to complete one turn about Earth's axis every 24 hours. We, on the other hand, would still have the same eastward velocity that we picked up at the equator. To us it would appear as if we were being deflected off course by an eastward directed force, but you can see that our eastward drift isn't the result of a force at all. The shell is simply keeping the eastward speed that it had at the line of latitude from which it was fired.

If we moved our cannon north of the equator and then aimed south, the situation would be reversed. Before we fired our shell, its eastward velocity would be the same as every other object located at that latitude. (As we've already pointed out, the higher the latitude we find ourselves, the slower we move about Earth's axis.) If we now fire our cannon due south (towards the equator), our shell will pass over lower and lower latitudes. The landscapes at these lower latitudes travel eastward at higher speeds than our shell. The lower the latitude, the faster they travel. Because our shell is still moving eastward at the rate it acquired when it was fired from the canon, it will look as if a force is deflecting us towards the west. We would drift eastward, away from our original line of longitude. Why? The world under us is speeding eastward faster than we are.

This curving effect—this apparent sideways-deflecting force—is so famous and so important that it even has its own special name. It's called the *Coriolis effect*. Sometimes its called the Coriolis force. But you can see that it's not a force at all. The Coriolis effect is just a consequence of moving north/south on a sphere that's spinning east/west.

The Coriolis effect is very important in understanding ocean currents. An Atlantic current moving north from the equator is deflected east toward Europe, and a current in the north Atlantic heading toward the equator is deflected west. This is just the Coriolis effect in action. Similarly, a current moving from the equator toward the South Pole is deflected east, while a current heading north toward the equator is deflected west.

Temperature and Currents

Under most conditions liquid water expands when heated and contracts when cooled. If we had a container of liquid water at 75° F (24° C), and we cooled it to 50° F (10° C) we'd find that the volume of the

Most of us know of Ben Franklin (1706-1790) as a scientist, inventor and American political leader. As a scientist he made several fundamental discoveries about electricity. As an inventor he invented the lightning rod and bifocal glasses among other things. In politics he was one of the leaders of the United States during the War of Independence and he helped write the Declaration of Independence.

Less well known is the fact that he was also Deputy Postmaster General for the colonies and, later, Postmaster General for the U.S. When he learned that it sometimes took as much as a month longer to deliver a letter from Britain to the United States than it took to deliver a letter from the United States to Britain, it was natural for him to investigate the cause. Even in the days of sailing ships a month was considered a very big difference. Why, he wondered, would the delivery times of transoceanic mail depend so much on the direction of delivery? He interviewed sailors and some of them explained to him the phenomena that we now call the Gulf Stream. (Not all sailors were familiar with the size, direction, and speed of the Gulf Stream.) During conversations with whalers he learned that whales were often found near the boundaries of the Gulf Stream but not inside it. The whalers sometimes followed the Gulf Stream and hunted along its boundaries. Sometimes, they sailed back and forth across it in search of their prey. They understood the size, shape and characteristics of what we now call the Gulf Stream.

From these sailors Ben Franklin learned that a captain of a mail ship that sailed with the Gulf Stream—that's the North America to Europe part of the circuit— could use the stream to propel the ship forward even when the winds were light or non-existent. Ships that sailed against the Gulf Stream—that's the Europe to North America part of the trip—would actually be pushed back toward Europe when the winds were light. Furthermore, even when the winds were strong enough to push them forward they made only slow progress toward North America because they were sailing "upstream."

water had shrunk. The change in volume is small, but with good equipment we could *measure* it. Just because the volume shrunk, however, doesn't mean there's less water in the container. The amount of water is unchanged. We know the amount of water is unchanged because the mass of the water is the same after we cooled it as it was

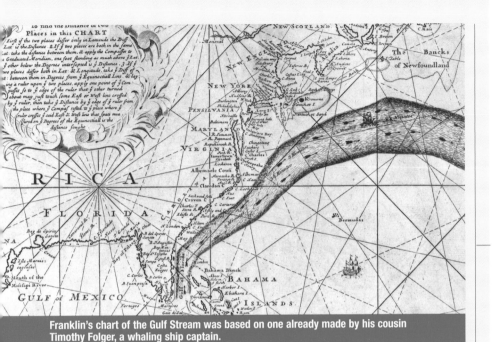

Franklin's chart of the Gulf Stream was based on one already made by his cousin Timothy Folger, a whaling ship captain.

Franklin recognized the importance of the Gulf Stream for mail delivery. He recognized that boats should sail with the stream on the way to Europe and avoid sailing into the stream on the return trip. To aid ship's captains and improve mail service he helped make one of the first maps of the Gulf Stream, which, when compared with modern images of the stream, can be seen to be remarkably accurate. Sailors and merchants greatly appreciated his work.

before we cooled it. Only the volume changed, so we know that the cooler water is more dense than the warmer water.

Now suppose that we had a tall cylinder of water. If we cooled only the water at the top of the cylinder—say we blew cool air across the top—the water would begin to contract. At this point we'd have a layer of cooler, denser water overlying a layer of warmer, less dense water. The warmer water at the bottom of the cylinder would not be able to support the denser water on the top and, under the influence of gravity, the denser water would gently flow down to the bottom of the cylinder.

These density-driven currents occur in the oceans, just as they occur in tall cylinders, but in a much bigger, more complex way. When billions of tons of water along the surface of the North Atlantic cool, they gently sink to the sea floor and begin to stream along the ocean basins. The precise path of the current is determined by the hills and valleys it encounters along the ocean floor and by the Coriolis effect. The current is further influenced by differences between the salt content of the current and the salt content of the surrounding water. (The concentration of salt in the water further alters its density.) This immense current is not visible from the surface. That's why it wasn't discovered until modern times. No one had even expected that a huge and powerful current flowed deep within the ocean basins. Its existence came as something of a surprise. So did its extent. This cold, bottom-hugging current begins in the North Atlantic and flows all the way around the world. It may take 1,000 years to complete its undersea, around-the-world journey. It's called the *thermohaline current* and it's one of the least understood of all the major ocean currents.

The Most Famous of the Open Ocean Currents

It's called the Gulf Stream.

Just north of the equator, in the southern part of the North Atlantic, winds blow from east to west. In the northern part of the

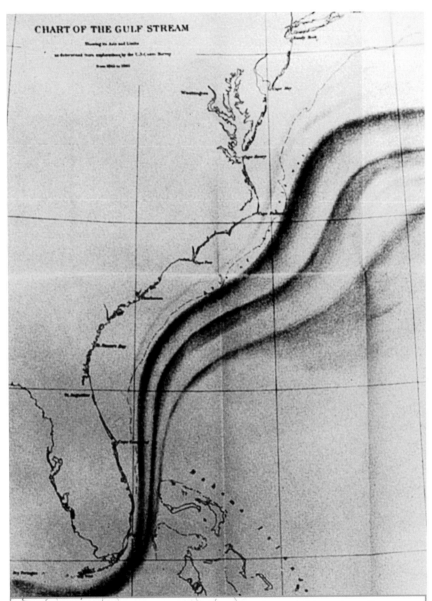

CHART OF THE GULF STREAM

This is an 1860 chart of the Gulf Stream, a current that flows along the western boundary of the North Atlantic Ocean. Today, the Gulf Stream is measured and charted using more advanced scientific techniques, such as sensors of ocean color, sea surface temperature measurement, and altimetry.

North Atlantic, winds blow from west to east. These winds cause a current that flows clockwise when viewed from space. Warm water from around Cuba flows north along the coast of the United States and then, as it passes North Carolina, this stream, the Gulf Stream, turns east toward Europe. The waters around Cuba are warm. They contain vast amounts of heat energy. As the Gulf Stream flows north it carries this heat energy along with it.

Eventually, the Gulf Stream crosses the Atlantic and divides into several branches. It's at this point that the Gulf Stream has, at least from the point of view of humanity, it's most important effect on the environment: it heats western Europe. This may seem like an exaggeration. It's not. Although Western Europe is a very big place, the Gulf Stream carries so much heat from the tropics that it heats the western part of an entire continent. The waters of the North Atlantic are cool. So is the air above the North Atlantic. When the warm waters of the Gulf Stream flow into this cooler environment, heat energy flows from the warm water into the cool air and surrounding water. The winds carry the warm air over Britain, France, Norway, Ireland and the other countries that border the North Atlantic.

To see the effect of the Gulf Stream on Western Europe you only need to compare winter temperatures on opposite sides of the Atlantic. Compare, for example, Cartwright, Canada, on the western side of the Atlantic, with Dublin, Ireland, on the eastern side of the Atlantic. Both are located at the latitude of about 57° N. (At these latitudes it's hard to make exact comparisons between cities. It's so cold on the western side of the Atlantic at 57° N that almost no one lives there.) The average minimum temperature in January in Cartwright is -1° F (-18° C) and the average maximum temperature in Cartwright in January is 15°

F (-9° C). In Dublin the average minimum temperature in January is 36° F (2° C) and the average maximum temperature in January is 46° F (8° C). The minimum temperature in January in Dublin is slightly above freezing, while the average maximum January temperature in Cartwright is well below freezing. Without the Gulf Stream the environment of Western Europe would be well suited to polar bears.

This image of Hurricane Linda swirling above the blue waters of the Pacific Ocean near the west coast of Mexico was taken by a U.S. weather satellite on September 12, 1997. The winds around the eye of the hurricane reached 190 miles (304 km) per hour, making it the strongest hurricane on record in the eastern Pacific.

Chapter 4

The Atmosphere

Most of the surface of our planet is liquid. About one-third of Earth's surface is land. All Earth's surface is submerged beneath miles of atmosphere. Sometimes we can see right through the entire atmosphere into outer space. Sometimes we can't. From space there are times when little of Earth's surface, liquid or solid, is visible. These are times when large areas of our large planet are hidden by enormous formations of swirling clouds. These clouds are in continual motion. They appear and disappear. In this chapter we'll learn how and why our atmosphere is in continual motion, and we'll learn about clouds. Like the thin streams of smoke that aerospace engineers use in wind tunnels to help them visualize how air flows over aircraft wings, clouds help us understand how air flows over Earth's surface. They are atmospheric motions made visible. We can learn a lot from clouds. First, however, we need to learn about air.

Air Chemistry

There's only one planet in the solar system whose atmosphere is mostly nitrogen. That's Earth. The chemical composition of every other planetary atmosphere in the solar system is very different from ours. Earth's atmosphere is about 80 percent nitrogen. Most of the rest is oxygen. There are also comparatively small amounts of argon, carbon dioxide, and a few other gases. But that's the chemical composition of dry air, air without water vapor. (Water vapor is water in gaseous form.)

Our atmosphere also contains water vapor. Unlike the chemical composition of dry air, which is pretty much the same everywhere on Earth, the amount of water vapor in the air varies a lot from place to place and from day to day. When water is in the form of vapor it can be transported through the atmosphere in large quantities all over the globe. Life on land is as dependent on water vapor as it is on liquid water, because before water can fall down in the form of rain, snow, hail, or sleet, it must first flow up in the form of vapor. During the monsoon season and during hurricanes (liquid) water pours down from the sky and floods the land. During blizzards (solid) water can cover the land in several feet of snow. All of that "atmospheric water" was at one time on the surface of the planet. All of it left the surface in the form of vapor.

Atmosphere and Ocean

Scientists describe both air and water as fluids because both air and water flow. Like the oceans, our fluid atmosphere is in continual motion. It can flow as delicately as a summer breeze or as violently as a hurricane, and, like the oceans, motion is the natural state of the atmosphere.

Clouds float above a rocky inlet on the coast of New Zealand. The high cliffs help deflect the wind, holding the clouds on the coast.

In many ways, the causes of motion in the atmosphere are the same as those in the seas. First, there's unequal heating of the atmosphere by the Sun. This happens in the atmosphere as well as the oceans and for many of the same reasons.

Second, the Coriolis effect influences the direction of large currents in the atmosphere just as it does large currents in the ocean. This is the reason that, when viewed from space, hurricanes rotate counterclockwise in the northern hemisphere and clockwise in the southern hemisphere. (See pages 60-62 for a discussion of the Coriolis effect.)

Finally, just as large-scale motions of the atmosphere cause surface currents to flow in the ocean, the ocean has an equally large influence on the atmosphere. We've already seen how the Gulf Stream, a large ocean current, affects air temperature over western Europe. Another example of the ocean affecting the atmosphere is hurricanes. Hurricanes form only over the ocean. As soon as a hurricane passes over land it begins to weaken and lose its spiral structure. The energy necessary to form and maintain a hurricane comes from the heat energy of the ocean beneath it.

In scientific language the oceans and atmosphere are often described as *coupled.* That means that it's hard to distinguish between a cause in one and an effect in the other. For example:

- Currents in the atmosphere can

- cause surface currents in the oceans, which, in turn, might

- transport heat to cooler regions, where

- the atmosphere is heated by the warmer ocean, which

- causes currents in the atmosphere, which

- cause currents in the oceans . . .

There's no end to it, and this makes it very difficult for scientists to develop accurate predictions about weather and climate. The atmosphere and ocean are so tightly coupled that we'll never really understand the motions of one until we understand the motions of both.

Heat and Motion

One of the big differences between the atmosphere and the oceans, a difference that's as important as it is simple, is that the atmosphere is heated from the bottom up, while the oceans are heated from the top down.

When the Sun shines on the oceans, it heats the top layers of water the most. The further down into the oceans we go the less sunlight there is. The bottom of every ocean basin is completely dark and quite cold.

In contrast with the ocean, air is transparent to sunlight. The Sun's rays pass right through the atmosphere. They pass through with little immediate effect on atmospheric temperature. (For example, six miles (10 km) above Earth's surface the temperature always hovers around –110° F (-79° C.)) Instead of heating the atmosphere on its way down, the Sun's light penetrates the entire atmosphere and strikes Earth's surface. The sunlight warms the surface, and *it's the surface that warms the air*. Heat flows from the surface into the air. This is true for air above land as well as for air above water. That's how, unlike the oceans, the atmosphere is warmed from below. Warming the atmosphere from below has a profound effect on how energy and matter are transported through the air.

The horizon falls away in the distance in this photograph taken from the cockpit of a glider plane. Like a hawk, a glider takes advantage of the unequal heating of Earth's surface by riding on thermals, or updrafts.

When air is heated it expands a lot. Water also expands when heated, but not nearly to the same extent. An increase of several degrees in the temperature of the atmosphere makes the air much less dense after heating than before. And because heating of the atmosphere occurs *at the planet's surface*, on a hot day the warmer, lighter air is at the bottom of the atmosphere. Piled high above it, is cooler, denser air. This makes the atmosphere very unstable: cooler, heavier air is pressing down on warmer, lighter air. That's why, during the day, huge masses of warm air push their way up through the denser regions of air above them and rise high into the atmosphere. In many ways they rise like those big, red and orange blobs in those lava lamps that were so popular during the 1960's.

Unfortunately, much of this process is invisible. Air is transparent. We can't look at it, we can only look through it. But if you've ever seen a hawk gliding in circles and soaring higher and higher without moving its wings, you now know what it's doing: it's riding one of these "vertical breezes."

Although the formation of thermals, which is what these rising air masses are sometimes called, is invisible, we can often see them once they rise high enough. We see them as they slow down and come to a stop. (They must eventually come to a stop because the atmosphere becomes less dense at higher altitudes. Eventually, the air outside the thermal is no denser than the air inside. The thermal eventually loses its buoyancy.) The last stages of these updrafts are sometimes visible as cumulus clouds. Clouds, as we noted earlier, are atmospheric currents made visible. We're now ready to understand why that's true.

Cloud Formation

On Earth, water is present in all three phases: solid, liquid, and vapor. This is part of what makes water special. Iron, for example, can exist in three phases, too, but near the surface of Earth, iron generally exists only as a solid. The phase in which we find water depends on temperature and pressure. Under certain conditions, water vapor, which is present in the air, condenses into tiny droplets. Sometimes it freezes into tiny ice crystals. These droplets and crystals can form clouds. Understanding how this occurs can help us appreciate how clouds reveal atmospheric motions. Here's a description of how a cumulus cloud might form near your home:

- Imagine the Sun warming a large patch of ground. The ground begins to heat the air. The air (including the water vapor!) warms up and expands. It becomes less dense than the air above it. This big mass of air and water vapor begins to rise into the atmosphere as if it were a big bubble. (All of this is invisible.)

- Now imagine that you could rise up into the atmosphere inside this bubble. As you left the ground behind you'd notice two things. First, there'd be a popping sensation in your ears. This is exactly what you experience when you ride an elevator up a tall building. It means that the air pressure in decreasing. Why? As the altitude increases, air pressure decreases. The next thing that you'd notice is that the temperature inside this rising bubble of air begins to decrease. You'd feel cooler, because as air rises it expands and loses heat energy. This loss of heat energy causes the temperature of the air to drop. Finally, you'd notice that the air felt increasingly damp. (As the temperature and pressure decrease, the water vapor gets closer and closer to the *dew point*, the point at which water vapor condenses into liquid water.)

- Finally, imagine that the air bubble in which you're rising gets high enough so that the dew point is reached. Then, suddenly, all

Cumulus clouds are characterized by vertical development from a flat base. The deepest cumulus clouds can be 20,000 feet (6,000 m) high and are known as cumulonimbus clouds. These are the clouds that are often seen before thunderstorms.

around you, small droplets of water begin to form. It's instant fog, but when it forms high in the atmosphere, we call it a cloud.

Notice that like the currents of liquid metal that churn away inside the outer core, and like the currents of rock that circulate through the upper and lower mantle, and like the deep, cold water currents that flow great distances along the ocean basins, these currents, the currents responsible for forming cumulus clouds, are also caused by density differences. In this case the differences occur between the warm air below and the cool air above.

Think back to all of those beautiful cumulus clouds that you've seen in the summer sky. They're all flat on the bottom and now you know why. Until the rising mass of air reaches a critical altitude, the water vapor inside the air mass isn't yet at the dew point. Underneath that altitude, the lower part of the rising air mass is still in motion but it's still transparent, too. It's rising, but because we can't see it we're usually not even aware that it's there. Above the critical altitude, the altitude at which the dew point is reached, water vapor continually changes into water droplets as the air mass rises higher and higher into the sky. A cumulus cloud is what we call that part of the rising air mass that's above the altitude where the water vapor begins to condense. The cloud is the visible part of the rising air mass!

Of course, there are other types of clouds. The idea behind their formation is, however, in many ways the same. *Altostratus* clouds, for example, can blot out the entire sky. These clouds look like a blanket suspended high over the entire landscape. They're formed by large-scale horizontal movements of air. Altostratus clouds develop when a very large mass of warmer, moist, less dense air, moving horizontally across the surface of the planet, encounters a mass of cooler, denser air. The warm air is deflected upward over the cool air, because it's more buoyant than the cooler air. As it rises into the sky the water vapor present in the air condenses and blots out the sky with an enormous blanket of clouds.

Global Warming

If there were no atmosphere the Sun would heat the surface of the planet during the day and that energy would radiate away into space at night. The atmosphere acts like a blanket. It doesn't retain all of the Sun's heat but it does retain some of it. How much heat the atmosphere retains depends on the chemical make-up of the atmosphere. Carbon dioxide gas is especially good at retaining heat energy.

There's only a little carbon dioxide gas in our atmosphere and most of it occurs naturally. It would be there even if we didn't burn fossil fuels. Some of the carbon dioxide presently in the atmosphere, however, can be traced directly to the burning of fossil fuels. (Fossil fuels include coal, heating oil, gasoline, natural gas, diesel and jet fuel.) Humans burn fossil fuels to stay warm in winter and cool in summer. We also use these fuels to heat our water, power our lights and computers and TVs, and to give our cars, trains, boats and planes the energy they need to go.

As we increase the level of carbon dioxide in the atmosphere our atmosphere will retain more heat from the Sun. There is, however, much uncertainty among scientists about how big a change in temperature will result as more and more carbon dioxide gas is added to the atmosphere. Scientists are busy collecting data to measure the changes that have already occurred.

To investigate the changes that have occurred in the atmosphere some scientists have placed extremely powerful loudspeakers in the oceans. They know that the speed of sound through water depends on the temperature of the water. In addition to the speakers they've also placed extremely sensitive receivers throughout the oceans. By regularly broadcasting sounds and measuring the time it takes for the sounds to travel across the oceans, they're able to monitor changes in average ocean temperature. It's a technique that enables them to detect even small changes in the average temperature of the oceans. This gives them insight into the extent of *global warming*, which is the name given to the gradual warming of Earth's atmosphere due to changes in atmospheric chemistry. These scientists monitor sounds in the oceans to gain insight into the changes we've caused in the atmosphere.

You can see how clouds tell us about the atmosphere's motion. They are the visible part of otherwise invisible air currents. They show those who know how to read them that Earth's atmosphere, like its oceans, its rocky surface and its interior, is a very dynamic place.

From Earth to Outer Space

Part of what makes our atmosphere so interesting and complicated is that there's so little of it. Earth's atmosphere is shallow and tenuous. It's wide in the sense that it covers the surface of our entire planet, but it's shallow in the sense that it goes from atmospheric pressures and temperatures at the surface to an almost perfect vacuum 100 miles (160 km) overhead. In fact, the atmosphere is compressed in such a way that most of the mass of the atmosphere lies in an extremely narrow region close to the surface of Earth. For example, the density of air about 11 miles (18 km) overhead is roughly a tenth of what it is at the surface.

A great cyclonic storm, as captured by a weather satellite. Scientists use the term cyclone to refer to a low pressure weather system that creates a violent, whirling windstorm.

Like the interior of our planet, Earth's atmosphere is stratified or organized into distinct regions. The bottom-most region, called the *troposphere*, contains most of Earth's weather. The troposphere is only about 6 miles (10 km) thick. Its height depends somewhat on latitude and time of year. The troposphere is characterized by a rapid drop in temperature with altitude. The specifics of the temperature drop depend on the latitude that we're considering but in temperate regions the temperature near the top of the troposphere hovers around -110° F (-79° C).

Above the troposphere is a region called the stratosphere. The air in the stratosphere is very thin—too thin to breath—but the stratosphere is important to life on Earth because it's in the stratosphere that we find the *ozone layer*. Ozone is a molecule formed by three oxygen atoms. Trace amounts of ozone can be found throughout the atmosphere, but the molecules are especially common in a layer of atmosphere that's roughly 12-19 miles (20-30 km) above Earth's surface. This region is called the ozone layer, although there are other kinds of gas in this region, because it's the ozone in which scientists have a particular interest. In the stratosphere ozone molecules act as a filter to prevent most of the Sun's ultraviolet light from reaching Earth's surface. This is important because ultraviolet light is harmful to life. We depend on the ozone layer to protect our health and the health of plants and animals all over the planet. (By the way, ozone at the surface of Earth is a pollutant. Breathing ozone eventually damages our health. It damages plants, too. Near Earth's surface ozone is a dangerous airborne chemical.) Above the stratosphere is a region called the ionosphere, and it's to the ionosphere that we now turn our attention.

The ionosphere is usually described as beginning about 30 miles (50 km) above Earth's surface. It extends upward hundreds of miles.

The atmosphere is extremely thin at these altitudes, and unlike the lower regions of Earth's atmosphere, the ionosphere is characterized by the presence of electrically charged particles called ions. Whether we describe this region as the uppermost region of our atmosphere or as the lowermost region of outer space depends on our point of view.

At certain frequencies radio waves will bounce off the ionosphere and return to Earth thousands of miles away from the point of transmission. International broadcasters like Radio Netherlands and Radio Canada International use the ionosphere to send their signals around the globe. On the other hand, some satellites orbit Earth inside the

In recent years, satellite imagery has become one of the most important tools for measuring change on Earth. This satellite image shows how quickly a particular section of the Brazilian rain forest is disappearing as a result of human activity.

ionosphere. So how we describe the ionosphere depends on the applications that we have in mind. The ionosphere is a wide region surrounding our planet where the atmosphere eventually ends and outer space eventually begins.

It's almost a perfect vacuum in the upper ionosphere. On the other hand there's enough matter left at even these very high altitudes to provide us with one of the most spectacular of all atmospheric phenomena, the *aurora*. (In the northern hemisphere it's called the aurora borealis. In the southern hemisphere it's called the aurora australis.) The appearance of an aurora depends on its intensity and the latitude at which we observe it. Sometimes they're unforgettable: great curtains of light ripple across the sky for hours, without generating a sound. Other times an aurora will appear as a delicate glow.

Aurora are the result of complicated interactions between the ionosphere, Earth's magnetic field, and the *solar wind*. The solar wind is what we call a stream of particles that flows outward from the Sun. This particle stream is composed of atoms and pieces of atoms called subatomic particles. Protons and electrons are examples of subatomic particles. The material that makes up the solar wind travels at about a million miles an hour, although the speed of the solar wind varies from day to day and so does its intensity. Some days the Sun ejects more mass than others.

Earth's magnetic field deflects most of the solar wind away from the planet, but some of the particles get trapped inside the magnetic field. Once inside, the magnetic field deflects the particles toward the North and South Poles. These high-energy particles, mostly electrons, collide with particles in the ionosphere and release energy in the form of light. This is the light that we observe as an aurora, and the more

The atmospheric phenomenon known as the aurora borealis, or northern lights, can be seen from the northernmost places on Earth.

powerful the solar wind, the bigger the aurora. In the northern hemisphere, during periods of high solar activity, aurora are occasionally visible as far south as 35° N. Normally, however, they're only visible near the poles. Aurora are a nice example of the interconnectivity of Earth's major systems. Flows of molten metal deep within Earth's outer core create a magnetic field that deflects the solar wind into a region high in the atmosphere to create an enormous light display that's visible from the surface. Aurora remind us that even on a calm, clear, peaceful night our planet is never still.

A look at Earth from space

Chapter 5

Harmony

The astronomer Johannes Kepler (1571-1630) was the first person to understand how planets move about the Sun. He spent most of his adult life working on the problem. At the time there were many people who still believed that everything—the Sun, the stars, and all of the planets—orbited Earth. In one of his books, *Harmony of the World*, Kepler concentrated on communicating the beauty of his discoveries. To Kepler, astronomy wasn't just a matter of discovering how the solar system was put together. He saw something more in his discoveries—something that he wanted to communicate—and so he turned to music. Each planet, he wrote, was like a single voice in a song written for several voices. The unique motion of each planet contributed to a harmonious whole. He called it, "the music of the spheres." In this way he tried to show others that while each planet followed its own path about the Sun, and each planet moved at its own speed, the result wasn't confusion. It wasn't noise. It was harmony.

I hope that this brief look at Earth has convinced you that although the motions inside and outside of our planet are very complicated—they are certainly more complicated than the motions that Kepler "heard"—the result isn't confusion. The motions that exist deep within Earth, the motions of its surface, the motions of its oceans and its atmosphere are all linked. Motions are piled upon motions are piled upon motions . . . and this makes for a very complex system. Everything, however, evolves together to produce a kind of harmony that only the scientifically curious can "hear." Our planet isn't so much a place as it is a process.

Earthly Comparisons

Vital Statistics

Category	Earth	Ranking (among other planets)
AVERAGE DISTANCE FROM THE SUN	150 billion km	3rd
MASS	5.97×1024	5th
DIAMETER	12.576 kg	5th
DENSITY	5.515 kg/m³	1st
LENGTH OF DAY	24 hours	5th
LENGTH OF YEAR	1 earth year	7th
MOONS	1	2nd fewest

Exploring Earth: A Timeline

1650-1749 — Johannes Kepler formulates his three laws of planetary motion.

Isaac Newton discovers the law of gravity, a discovery that allows scientists to calculate the mass of an object by measuring the strength of its gravitational pull.

1750-1799 — Benjamin Franklin publishes the first map of the Gulf Stream.

James Hutton publishes theory and evidence that the world is much older than previously believed.

1800-1849 — Charles Darwin's book *The Voyage of the Beagle* is first published.

Evidence begins to accumulate for the existence of the Mid-Atlantic Ridge.

1850-1899 — William Thomson (Lord Kelvin) uses a mathematical model of heat conduction to estimate the age of Earth.

United States Geological Survey, USGS, is founded in 1879.

1900-1949 — Marie Curie isolates radioactive substances and begins an experimental investigation of their physical properties. This leads to a reliable method for finding the age of Earth and also explains much of the inaccuracy in Lord Kelvin's estimate of Earth's age.

The first accurate, reliable seismometer is invented by Emil Weichert.

Alfred Wegener develops a theory and evidence to show that the continents are in motion.

1950-1999 — Soviet Union launches *Sputnik*, the first artificial satellite, in 1957. The Space Age begins.

During the International Geophysical Year (July '57-December '58), scientists from 67 countries cooperate in the study of Earth's geology, oceans, and atmosphere. One of the most successful of all such undertakings, its results will later be used

to establish, among other things, the cause of auroras and the theory of plate tectonics.

National Aeronautics and Space Administration, NASA, is founded in 1958.

Powerful new evidence of the motion of the continents is discovered in sonar and magnetic measurements made along the floor of the Atlantic Ocean. The theory of plate tectonics is firmly established.

The United States National Oceanic and Atmospheric Administration, NOAA, is founded in 1970.

In 1970 the Soviet Union begins to drill what will prove to be the deepest hole ever made in the surface of the Earth. The program is ended in 1989 at a depth of 7.4 miles (12 km). The temperature at the bottom of the hole is 370° Fahrenheit (190° C).

In 1996 the theory that Earth's core rotates faster than the surface is first proposed, an idea that has attracted the attention of many scientists as well as a lot of controversy.

In 1997 El Nino, a periodic warming of a large area of the Pacific Ocean, recurs with unusual severity, affecting weather around the globe. Scientists take advantage of this unusual opportunity to study the coupling of the oceans and atmosphere.

2000– Computer simulations of Earth's interior, its oceans, and atmosphere play an ever more prominent role in our understanding of Earth's interior. The computations become increasingly ambitious as scientists seek to test their mathematical models against the data. Most government research agencies and academic institutions are now engaged in large-scale modeling of planet Earth.

Glossary

altostratus cloud—continuous cloud cover that forms when a warm, moist air mass is deflected upward over a denser, cooler air mass.

aurora—a phenomena that occurs when high energy particles from the Sun interact with Earth's ionosphere. Aurora are marked by sheets of light in the night sky. They are usually visible only from the upper latitudes.

continental shelf—the narrow submerged margin of a continent. The continental shelf slopes gradually away from the continent beneath the sea.

Coriolis effect—(also called Coriolis force) an apparent deflecting force resulting from Earth's rotation.

coupled systems—Systems that cannot evolve independently of one another.

cumulus cloud—a cloud with a flat base and a fluffy, rounded top.

density—the ratio of an object's mass to its volume. Density is a way of describing how closely packed a group of atoms or molecules are—the more closely they're packed, the higher their density.

density-driven currents—currents that arise due to buoyancy effects. Density differences in the medium result in the less dense, more buoyant material flowing upward.

dew point—For a given pressure the dew point is the temperature at which water vapor condenses.

global warming—the gradual warming of Earth's atmosphere and oceans due to changes in the chemistry of the atmosphere.

Gulf Stream—a current of warm water that flows north from Cuba along the coast of the southeast U.S. and then eastward toward the shores of western Europe.

inner core—the region at the center of Earth composed mostly of solid iron.

ionosphere—the region of Earth's atmosphere beginning about 30 miles (50 km) above Earth's surface. It is marked by extremely low atmospheric densities and the presence of continually changing layers of charged particles, called ions.

lower mantle—A thick spherical region inside Earth that encloses the (liquid) outer core and is, in turn, enclosed by the upper mantle.

mass—the quantity of material in a body.

Mid-Atlantic Ridge—the volcanic mountain chain that bisects the Atlantic Ocean and is the site of sea floor spreading.

outer core—the region enclosing the inner core. It is composed mostly of molten iron and nickel and is, in turn, enclosed by the lower mantle.

ozone—a molecule consisting of three oxygen atoms.

ozone layer—a region in the upper atmosphere where ozone has a relatively high concentration. The ozone layer blocks much of the Sun's ultraviolet light from reaching the surface.

plate tectonics—the scientific theory that asserts that Earth's surface is composed of plates that scrape and collide with one another as they move.

radioactivity—the property of certain atoms to spontaneously break apart and in the process emit heat and subatomic particles.

seismometer—a device used to measure the location and intensity of earthquakes.

solar wind—a stream of atomic and subatomic particles that flows outward from the Sun in all directions.

stratosphere—the region of Earth between the troposphere and the ionosphere. The stratosphere contains the ozone layer.

subduction zone—an area where one of Earth's crustal plates is overridden by another.

thermohaline current—a globe-girdling, deep-water, density-driven ocean current.

troposphere—the region of Earth's atmosphere closest to the surface. The troposphere contains most of Earth's weather and is marked by a steady drop in temperature to an altitude of about 6 miles (10 km), where the troposphere ends and the stratosphere begins.

upper mantle—the region of Earth's interior that is directly below the crustal plates and above the lower mantle.

To Find Out More

The news from space changes fast, so it's always a good idea to check the copyright date on books, CD-ROMs, and videotapes to make sure that you are getting up-to-date information. One good place to look for current information from NASA, the National Oceanic and Atmospheric Administration (NOAA) and the U.S. Geological Survey (USGS) is U.S. government depository libraries. There at least one in each state.

BOOKS

Audubon Society Staff, *Clouds and Storms.* New York: Alfred A. Knopf, Inc., 1995

Barr, George, *Outdoor Science Projects for Young People.* New York: Dover Publications, Inc., 1959

Darwin, Charles, *The Voyage of the Beagle.* New York: Doubleday & Co., 1962

Dickinson, Terrence, *Exploring the Sky by Day, The Equinox Guide to Weather and the Atmosphere.* Ontario: Camden House Publishing, 1988

Kious, Jacquelyne and Tilling, Robert, *This Dynamic Earth: The Story of Plate Tectonics.* available as an online book from the U.S. Geological Survey *http://pubs.usgs.gov/publications/text/dynamic.html* 1996

Lauber, Patricia, *Seeing Earth From Space.* New York: Orchard Books, 1990

The Lawrence Hall of Science at the University of California at Berkeley Staff, *Energy.* available online, *http://www.lhs.berkeley.edu/GSS/OrderGSS-textware.pdf* 1995

Patent, Dorothy Hinshaw and Muñoz, William, *Shaping The Earth.* New York: Clarion Books, 2000

VanCleave, Janice, *Astronomy for Every Kid: 101 Easy Experiments that Really Work.* New York: John Wiley and Sons, 1991.

Walker, Sally, *Water Up, Water Down: The Hydrogeologic Cycle.* Minneapolis, MN: Carolrhoda Books, Inc., 1992

Websites/Organizations

Aurora Websites

To see some stunning pictures of aurora, see the site maintained by the San Francisco museum, The Exploratorium.
http://www.exploratorium.edu/learning_studio/auroras/
To read a paper about the science of aurora, see a website maintained by the National Oceanographic and Atmospheric Administration at *http://www.sec.noaa.gov/info/Aurora.pdf*

Earth Observing System

http://eospso.gsfc.nasa.gov
This website describes NASA's program to explore Earth *as a single system* from outer space. It's very interesting.

The National Aeronautics and Space Administration (NASA)

http://www.earth.nasa.gov
NASA is an excellent reference for planet Earth. This is another of their websites devoted to Earth.

The National Geographic Society

http://www.nationalgeographic.com/
The National Geographic Society produces a beautiful magazine with many interesting articles on various aspects of planet Earth. The society supports research and exploration around the world, and it has an excellent website.

The National Oceanic and Atmospheric Administration (NOAA)
www.noaa.gov
NOAA is a great source of information. Its website is well-organized and very accessible. It provides lots of information on the atmosphere and the oceans and real-time views of Earth from space.

Scientific American
http://www.sciam.com/askexpert_directory.cfm
Scientific American is one of the great science magazines written for a general audience. In addition to the magazine, *Scientific American* also provides an "Ask an Expert" website that provides interesting answers to fascinating questions. Find it at the website given above.

The Smithsonian Institution
http://seawifs.fsfs.nasa.gov/OCEAN_PLANET/HTML/ocean_planet_overview.html
The Smithsonian had a wonderful exhibit on the oceans entitled *Ocean Planet*. The exhibit is gone now except for the virtual version, which is available at the above website.

The United States Geological Survey (USGS)
http://geology.er.usgs.gov/eastern/inquiries.html
The USGS has more maps than any two people could ever look at, as well as lots of information about volcanoes, earthquakes, plate tectonics, and other important geological phenomena.

Places to Visit

The best places to go to learn about planet Earth (in addition to your local library) are science museums. Find the science museums nearest you and take time to visit them all. The United States and Canada, for example, have many high quality science museums. Here's a short list of some good ones:

American Museum of Natural History
Hall of Planet Earth
Central Park West at 79th St.
New York, NY 10024-5192
http://www.amnh.org/museum

Center of Science and Technology
333 West Broadway Street
Columbus, OH 43215
www.cosi.org/
A very interesting museum with many creative exhibits. After you've seen some of the exhibits take a ride on the high-wire unicycle!

Discovery Place
301 North Tryon Street
Charlotte, NC 28202
www.discoveryplace.org/
Wide ranging and creative exhibits.

The Exploratorium
3601 Lyon Street
San Francisco, CA 94123
http://www.exploratorium.edu/
This is a famous museum with a wide variety of high-quality exhibits.

Houston Museum of Natural Science
1 Hermann Loop Drive
Houston, TX 77030
www.hmns.org/
The museum has an astronomical observatory that's open to the public. The George Observatory is located in Brazos Bend State Park, with regularly scheduled times for public viewing.

The Montshire Museum
1 Montshire Road
Norwich, VT 05055
www.montshire.net/
This is a small, creative, high-quality, hands-on science museum.

The Museum of Science
Science Park
Boston, MA 02114
www.mos.org/
This museum takes many well-spent days to explore.

The National Museum of Science and Technology
1867 St. Laurent Blvd.
Ottawa, Ontario K1G 5A3
Canada.
http://www.science-tech.nmstc.ca/
A huge museum with many excellent exhibits.

The National Air and Space Museum
Washington, D.C. 20560-0321
www.nasm.si.edu
Part of the Smithsonian Institution, this is one of the great museums of its kind in the world. Take time to see the permanent exhibit entitled Looking@Earth.

Odyssium
11211-142 Street
Edmonton, Alberta T5M 4A1
Canada
www.odyssium.com/
This museum has undergone a lot of changes over the years. It keeps getting better.

Radioactivity, 22, 24

Satellites, 29, 54, 81–82
Secondary waves *See* S waves
Seismometers, 16, 17–18
Shadow zone, 16
Shear waves *See* S waves
Silicon, 35
Snowy Mountains, 39
Solar system, 11, 18, 29, 68,
    85–86
Solar wind, 82–83
South magnetic pole, 26, 28
Soviet Union, 38
Stratosphere, 80
Subatomic particles, 82
Subduction zones, 46–47, 52
Sun, 11, 70, 71, 74, 82

Surface currents, 54, 61–65
    causes of, 56
S waves, 16

Thermals, 72–73
Thermohaline current, 63
Thomson, William *See* Kelvin,
    Lord
Troposhere, 80

Ultraviolet light, 80

Volcanoes, **20**, 21. 47
Voyage of the Beagle, The (Dar-
    win), 40

Water vapor, 68, 74, 76, 77
Wegener, Alfred, 43–44

About the Author

John Tabak has a Ph.D. in mathematics and lives in Essex Junction, VT, with his beautiful wife, Gail, and their children, Leo and Leela. As a radio amateur his voice can sometimes be heard bouncing off the ionosphere.

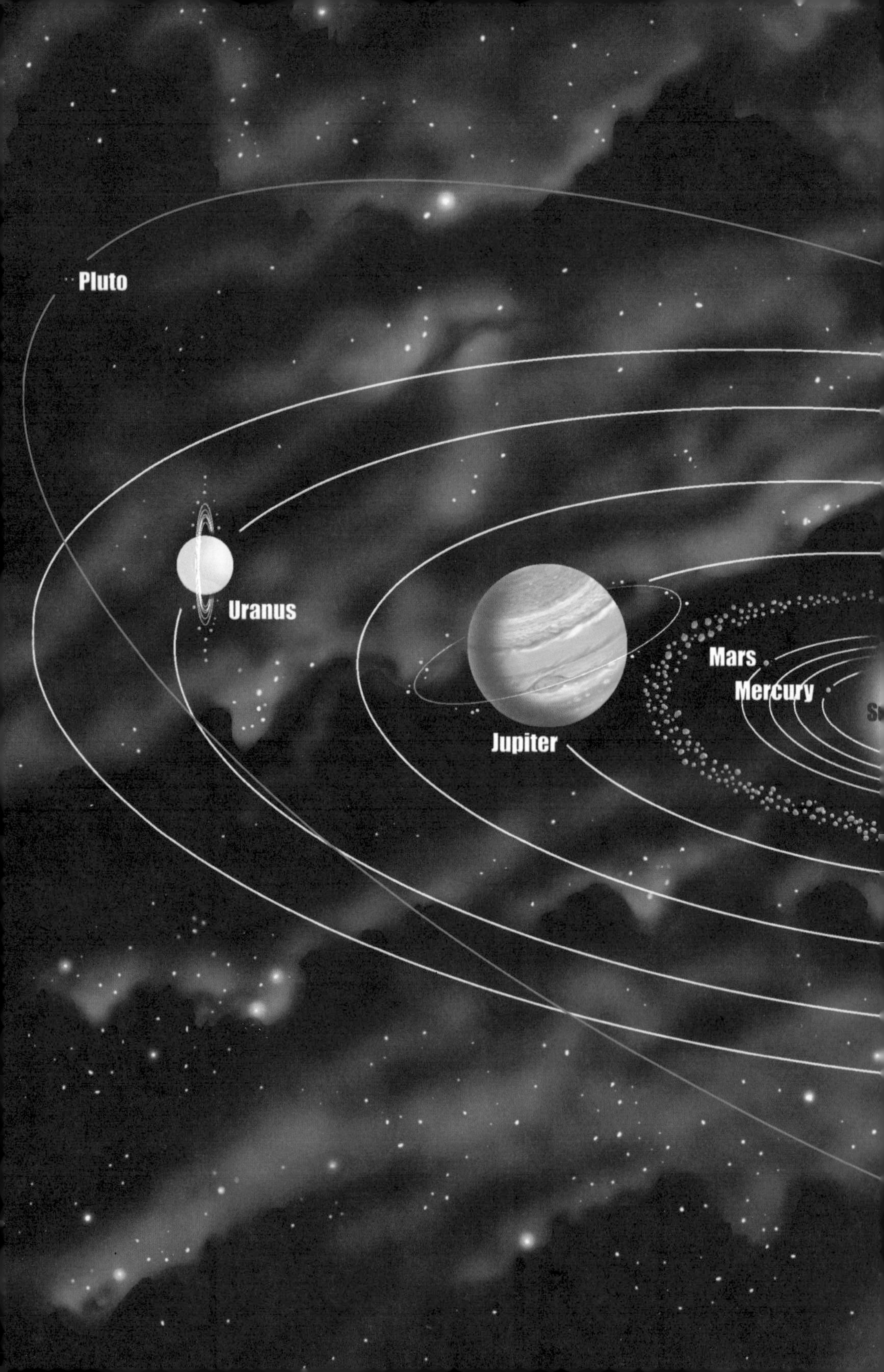
Pluto
Uranus
Jupiter
Mars
Mercury